THE EMPTY CHAIR

poems by

James Miller Robinson

Finishing Line Press
Georgetown, Kentucky

THE EMPTY CHAIR

Copyright © 2021 by James Miller Robinson
ISBN 978-1-64662-421-8 First Edition
All rights reserved under International and Pan-American Copyright Conventions. No part of this book may be reproduced in any manner whatsoever without written permission from the publisher, except in the case of brief quotations embodied in critical articles and reviews.

ACKNOWLEDGMENTS

Acknowledgements: Gratitude to the Magazines and Journals where some of these poems first appeared:

Back at the University in *Birmingham Arts Journal*
Café La Habana in Mexico City in *Coffee Poems: reflections on life with coffee*
Uncle Perry's Clothes in *Kaleidescope*
Pesos in *LUNA*
First Class with Everette Maddox in *Maple Leaf Rag VI: An Anthology of Poetic Writings from New Orleans*
Walking the Streets of Asheville with Thomas Wolfe at My Side; At Riverside Cemetery in Asheville in *Magic: Thomas Wolfe Society Anthology of Poetry*
Agnes in *POEM*
The School of Fish in *Red and Blue*: The Student Newspaper of Huntsville High School
The Book of Mormon in *Southern Humanities Review*
The Same Table in *Texas Review*
At Big Spring Park in *Whatever Remembers Us: An Anthology of Alabama Poetry*
What the Preacher Says in *WIND Magazine*
Hope in *Windhover: A Journal of Christian Literature*
At Lowe Mill; The Marionette Tango in San Telmo in *Xavier Review*

Publisher: Leah Huete de Maines
Editor: Christen Kincaid
Cover Art: Isidro Robinson
Author Photo: Isidro Robinson
Cover Design: Elizabeth Maines McCleavy

Order online: www.finishinglinepress.com
also available on amazon.com

Author inquiries and mail orders:
Finishing Line Press
PO Box 1626
Georgetown, Kentucky 40324
USA

Table of Contents

Agnes 1
At Big Spring Park 3
At Lowe Mill 4
Lowe Mill Late in the Afternoon 6
Back at the University 7
First Class with Everette Maddox 8
Walking the Streets of Asheville with Thomas Wolfe at My Side ... 9
At Riverside Cemetery in Asheville 10
With Jacqueline Smith at the Lorraine Motel 11
On Magazine Street 13
Uncle Perry's Clothes 14
What the Preacher Says 16
The Book of Mormon 17
Pesos 18
The Empty Space at the Head of the Table 20
The Salvatorian 21
The School of Fish 23
My Grandparents Gaze 24
The Trail 25
Hope 26
The Marionette Tango in San Telmo 27
Darkness Falls 29
Café La Habana in Mexico City 30
Coyoacán 31
The Perfect Place to Live in New Orleans 32
The Same Table 33

AGNES

The farmhouse still stands
on a stretch of rocky land,
an opening in the woods
of middle Tennessee—a place
you have to go on purpose,
no accident would lead you there.
You have to know the highway,
then which turn to make
and where to turn again.
It was no accident,
though the purpose today
is no more clear
than it was that day
Pa Parsons sent his brother
for the doctor and the aunts
who'd know what was to be done
while he waited on the porch
and watched the sun climb
above the cedar trees
on the horizon across the road.
It seemed it would keep going
and never curve into its arch.
Not a cow bellowed, only birds
chirping from fence posts
and trees, and the movement
inside the house whose meaning
he couldn't begin to fathom.
The sun finally made its curve
until it hung straight above.
They called him in and told him
to have a look at his baby girl.
The mother lay asleep, exhausted.
It hadn't been an easy thing,
but she had done it.

That little red face was round
as the sun, and it shone.
Now, later and miles away,
she lies in bed again.
Her cold white face
lies silent as the moon.

AT BIG SPRING PARK

An empty picnic table sits beside the clear
slow-moving current of Indian Creek cotton canal
with its stone walls shaped and placed by slaves
two hundred years ago
when a handful of planters, brokers, and bankers
saw the need to expedite the loading of their bales
onto steamboats at the Tennessee River ten miles away.
It took hundreds of them
with shovels and picks keeping time
with mournful songs and buckets full of dirt and sweat
eleven years to complete the project
with dozens of long-eared mules hitched to wagons
half-asleep and staring down between blinders
at the chip and crack of iron and rock.
It took half a century more to erect the blocks
of mansions that sprouted along the cobblestone streets
behind white columns, closed windows and thick doors.
A hundred years later they landscaped a park
around the squirting spring and along the banks
of the canal all the way to the rounded ponds it feeds.
They brought white geese, ducks and swans to glide
like angels across the crystal surface of dark water.
The giant carp they stocked grew
and multiplied amid bundling water weed.
Unforgetting willow trees sprouted up
to weep and sway at the edges of the ponds.
If you listen hard when traffic subsides
and chirping birds roost
in the upper branches of the trees,
you can still hear the mournful sound
of slaves shifting shovels back and forth,
lifting iron picks and slamming them down.

AT LOWE MILL

A fortress of high brick walls with rows
of tall paned windows surrounds wood floors
as long and broad as football fields.
Rows of fluorescent lights hang by chains
from ceilings intersected with water pipes,
sewer lines, and electrical conduit.

Each floor has four small restrooms,
a toilet, a urinal, and a sink
where workers—adults as well as children—
had to ask permission to go
between scheduled breaks and lunchtime.
There were long tables and benches at one end
of each vast floor where they ate what they brought
in metal boxes or tin pails and tried to talk
in spite of the rattle and shuffle of a hundred looms
and spinning machines.
                          A gossamer haze
of cotton fiber hovered in the noisy air.
No one knew what brown lung was
until years later it was given a name.
Tuberculosis and emphysema sneaked like mice
into the buildings between workers' feet.

There were baseball leagues, softball and basketball,
in which sections of the mill and other mills
could joust each other to show their pride,
loyalty and sense of belonging.

Workers came and gathered from the hopelessness
of the countryside at the changing of the centuries
and during the depression.
They lived in rows of wooden houses
—some duplexes, some shot-gun shacks, some
two-story quadraplexes with concrete latrines
along alleys between back yards where
chickens roamed amid small gardens planted
as much to remind of lost country homes
as for the food they could no longer buy
on credit at the company store.

The rackety looms and spinning machines
have been lifted up and carried off
to other plants in hungrier countries now.
The fiber fog has drifted away, settled, or been washed
from memory. The cages that once lifted bales
of cotton and descended with pallets of stacked cloth
stand empty and stopped between floors.
The rusting water tank still overlooks the empty castle
and surrounding blocks of dilapidated houses
like a penitentiary tower.

LOWE MILL LATE IN THE AFTERNOON
—*for Everett Carter*

In the afternoon emptiness of the third floor
at the hour when daylight fades
and yellow streetlights glow
on surrounding streets,
the windows of the village houses ignite
like weak votive candles not quite sure
whether to proclaim their light
or close their eyes in disbelief and die.
Anyone still in the studios
can hear a pair of approaching shoes
from any corner of the field-size floor
as loose oiled boards creak
and make you think of the combat boots
that marched through jungles and trudged
across saturated rice paddies in Vietnam
and the streets and sidewalks of Saigon,
all cut out, sewn together on noisy iron,
and vulcanized in steam with thick rubber soles
by the workers of Genesco Shoe
filling contracts for the Army and Marines,
many of whom did not come home.
Almost forgotten now, their faces fade
between the palpitating stars as darkness falls.

BACK AT THE UNIVERSITY

In Ferguson cafeteria
I glimpse
from the corner of one eye
the black
of a thin man's suit coat
several tables away
across the years
and think
for one absurd instant
it's Everette Maddox
bowed over a book of Berryman,
sipping coffee from a Styrofoam cup,
letting his thoughts play
with the sly and melancholy
before he goes to teach a class.
It is when he was still on fire
with possibility and promise
with recent poems
in *The New Yorker* and *Paris Review*,
before he left for New Orleans
and propped himself on a stool
at the Maple Leaf where
they dubbed him "the professor"
as he presided over poetry
readings in the courtyard
where the granite marker
and bronze plaque
that bear his name
and the epitaph lie flat
beneath dusty leaves
of tropical tress,
before darkness settled in
and he was consumed,
never to return.
I even catch a whiff
of the incense of his pipe,
and am absolutely sure I see
a question mark of smoke
hovering above the empty chair.

FIRST CLASS WITH EVERETTE MADDOX

It must have been
in one of the older
buildings that replaced
the ones burned down
during the Civil War
beneath the Druid oaks
in the central quad.
Since it was January
the vested wool suit
did not seem out of place
nor the old-timey beard,
but the chrome-colored
aluminum rack adhesive-taped
to his forehead, upper cheeks
and nose with rubber tube
looped into one nostril
beneath the votive candles
of his blackened eyes
could not have been
more strange than his lack
of any explanation
until after an hour and minutes
before we were dispersed
he finally addressed the issue
that had held us in suspense
by waving an open hand
before his afflicted face,
"Oh, this? Don't mind this.
This is just what happens
when you mix a little darkness
with a lot of Scotch."

WALKING THE STREETS OF ASHEVILLE
WITH THOMAS WOLFE AT MY SIDE

The facades of the buildings you once knew
still stand along the hilly blocks of streets
now transformed from banks,
hotels and department stores
into restaurants, cafés, antique shops, boutiques
and junk stores that cater to those
who pass through and all but ridicule
the world of a century ago you described
nestled between the wooded mountains
promising rest to the weary and broken-hearted.

Now they are the wandering lost
who never quite embark
on their impulsive trek
across the Appalachian Trail,
students who come on a summer off
and never get around to going back,
retired men who at the urging of their wives
arrive to fill the empty space
between Boston, New York, Philadelphia,
and Miami, Palm Beach, or Sarasota.

The marble angel on the porch
is just a misty shadow now, a ghost
still gazing off beyond the hills
where you went away in search of home,
leaving it behind.

The sons and daughters of Dixieland boarders,
their children, grandchildren, great grandchildren,
keep coming year after year,
returning to the home you relinquished.
The sidewalks of Asheville and the corners of its streets
grow crowded with yearning and littered with loss.

AT RIVERSIDE CEMETERY

A narrow road weaves between
eighty sloping acres of grass and trees.
Nine thousand monuments gather
in a diverse congregation of women and men
lying quiet as though asleep
among an interspersing of sitting lambs
and standing angels huddled inside folded wings
and gazing with darkened marble eyes
toward another world beyond the hills.
Irregular terraced rows of graves
rest along the slopes, a few
above ground in ivy-covered mausoleums
beneath the shade of giant oaks
like small Roman temples
where variations of "Romeo and Juliet"
might be acted out by casts of Thespian ghosts.

Beside a set of mossy stone-block stairs,
William Sydney Porter snickers
at this own surprising end,
no longer hiding behind his pseudonym,
his wife and daughter finally at his side.
On a dark and shady plot higher up the slope
Thomas Wolfe lies among his brothers
who came so early to this place,
his sisters, his beloved mother, and cold father.

He broods perpetually in guilt and sorrow
at how even their gravestones wear
the fictional names in which they were disguised
in the more-lasting monument of his novels.
Even though dozens of graves along sloping acres
hold the perched and leaning slabs of stone
his father cut, chizzled, engraved and polished,
or the Italian sculptures he sold a hundred years ago,
not a single marble angel
hovers above his own family's crowded space.

WITH JACQUELINE SMITH AT THE LORRAINE MOTEL

On the balcony hang a couple of wreaths,
a few signs to identify the room
and his picture inside glass, a shrine.
But almost everyone who drives by
finds your plastic tarpaulin encampment
outside the chain-link fence below
where Dr. King spent his last night
repugnant.

              You say this is your home.
This the place you lived and worked
before they came and carried you out
and left you here beside your furniture
on the sidewalk to take your own stand
"in protest of the exploitation of this site."

Speakers blare recorded speeches and sermons.
They bounce off the walls of vacant buildings.
What is it like to hear these words
over and over for all these years?
What is it like to try to keep the dream alive
when you can hardly sleep?

Maybe you're right.
Maybe a shelter for the homeless
would be a more fitting memorial.
Maybe a poor people's clinic would better serve.
But there are tourist dollars to be reaped.

Graceland brings millions to the city
as tour buses fill with fans
who believe another king lives on.
They seldom pass the Lorraine to see, just
so they can say they did, the place where
the voice in the wilderness was silenced.

You say they want to make it a circus
and a laser beam to trace the bullet's path
might appeal to less-noble curiosities, but
are grotesque poverty and need the proper nests
in which to lay the martyr's memory?

In your early stubborn days many claimed
to agree. Newspapers voiced your sobs.
Photocopies wait like empty plates on a table
along with other relics beneath the speakers.
But the years trudge on, support wanes
and tourists glance through tinted glass
with no recognition of your cause
and no understanding.

Now even the once-fervent question your sanity.
The streets of Memphis have changed, Jacqueline.
There are renewal projects and tourists to consider.
Even Beale Street bleeds empty of the blues.

ON MAGAZINE STREET

It's good to walk again
past the houses and the shops,
the outboard-motor sound of window units
churning through the summer mug,
the hardware store stuffed and full,
the chocolate shop, the *taquería*,
coffee houses and neighborhood bars,
the sidewalk crowded with tables and chairs
in front of po'boy shacks and pizzerias,
parked cars lined on both sides,
a slow-moving caravan in between,
elegant churches and casual bars
balancing the neighborhoods
in this constant sense of reconstruction,
remodeling, reconsideration and renewal,
where the flaking gray boards of even
the most dilapidated homes will
be reinforced, repainted and renewed.
Every century-and-a-half old house,
huddled side-by-side, has its porch
peeking from behind camellias and palms,
elephant ears and banana leaves
—some, balconies on second floors,
two, three, or four front doors,
low wrought-iron fences,
locked gates, and yapping dogs.
It's good to be back beneath
the low branches of the oaks,
stepping between thick tentacles of roots
oozing up from beneath cracked sidewalks.
The full moon glows
through purple haze above triangular roofs
like the glass globes on posts
at the corners of principal streets
where Mardi Gras beads sparkle from the leaves
even though the stench of the deluge
still simmers in the steam.

UNCLE PERRY'S CLOTHES

Dependent on his mother
for almost everything until she died
when he himself was seventy-five,
his was not the kind of life
many would think to follow.
And his life's work was not the kind
many would intend to attain:
custodian of a grammar school
in a community so small every one knew
everything about everybody else,
who owned land and who didn't,
who was who for generations back,
and of course,
all the kids—decades of them—knew
he wasn't quite at their disposal.

He held his head at an awkward tilt
trying to see through his "good" eye,
missing spots on the floors he waxed,
unable to tell by himself
if his pants and shirts
were clean enough to wear again
or needed to be washed, and which
pants and shirts went together well.
Whenever he settled on an acceptable match
he kept them hung on the same hanger.
And these are the pants and shirts
I'm rummaging through now to see
if any are worth keeping.

There are empty packs
of *Bull-of-the-Woods* in the pockets.
More than half the pants the same
khaki, olive green or gray,
the custodian's uniform
because he was proud to have a job,
having survived the depression and years
of boarding at the state institute
where he learned
any job was a "good" job.

They are about my size.
Every shirt's print years out of fashion.
But I'll take these few things
Uncle Perry had to give
and even if I don't wear them
they'll hang in my closet for me
to see every morning in a rush
when I jerk through the hangers in the dark—
more feeling than seeing—
trying to decide what image to wrap myself in
for another day at a different school
but a school just the same.
Maybe I'd be better off
carrying a mop bucket and a broom
rather than my briefcase full of worry.

Someday I might find a match
buried here between the hangers
and my own out-dated garb. I'll dress
myself in the few things he possessed.
Sleeve by sleeve, leg by leg,
I'll step into his shadow,
hold my own head at an awkward tilt,
squint my eyes until I see,
then stagger out to face the world,
still unsure but true,
with Uncle Perry's help to find the way
through darkening corridors and empty rooms.

WHAT THE PREACHER SAYS

Unpainted barns and wooded hills break
the monotony of cotton fields and cows.
The dark stones of a graveyard
perch on the nearest crest.
In a grove of autumn trees, a white
frame church with drooping roof stands
on limestone boulders at its base.
"Upon these rocks I build my church,"
a preacher may have said when
this meeting house was conjured up
a century and a half ago. Women
spread cloths on long board tables
as men stand around a water barrel
with a coffee percolator at its side.
A few in starched white shirts walk
back from the outhouse in the yard
while the rest file in and take
a seat on straight-back pews
within bare walls and a musty smell.
Hymns somehow harmonize and pour
out the windows loud and strong.
A deacon prays down on his knees
—lots of *Thee's* and *Thy's*.
Another stanza of "Amazing Grace"
as the preacher takes the stand.
He says, *His little ones will show*
like they have since times of old.
Not by what they say but what they are.
Like hot grease in a dry gourd dipper:
what's on the inside is going to show.
Like red cedar fence posts planted deep
to stand a long time: almost all heart.
Some nod and groan to show they agree.
Others stare out or doze off to sleep.
Children crawl beneath pews or doodle in
the margin of a hymnal's yellowed page.
Only a few care one way or the other
but what's on the inside shows through.

THE BOOK OF MORMON

Ten years since
any white trash
lived in this shack
all but hidden
in the overgrowth,
we weave through weeds,
briars and Johnson grass,
then Aunt Mary and I
crop across the porch
and squeak the hinges
that open a door,
reluctant and stiff,
like uneasy memories
too close at hand.
Clothes and single shoes
litter the floor.
Pages of molded magazines.
A soiled mattress,
stuffing hanging out.
Dusty toys and broken dolls.
"Must have got run off,"
guesses Aunt Mary as we
nudge through the rummage.
She picks up a rusty iron,
then a tea kettle
with the handle gone.
A leather-backed book
catches my eye
—looks like a Bible.
Beneath the dust
a figure etched in gold:
trumpet raised to mouth.
Foreign mysteries come to mind:
Hindus, Muslims, and ancient Hebrews.
Then I think of gypsy hicks
loading an old Ford
to move from shack to shack
in a perpetual search
of modern day saints.

PESOS

When the peso fell
and it took hundreds to buy a dollar,
we sold off the furniture,
gave away the dogs,
boxed up toys and books to send by freight,
then packed our suitcases, the typewriter
and everything else we could squeeze in
or strap to the roof of the Volkswagen
and headed back north
where we were able to cross
everything at Laredo but the car.
It took all day to find
someone on the southern side able
and willing to take it off our hands
and pay a half-decent price in dollars
because the peso now was no more use.
We carried with us a quart jar full
because Ani like to play with them.
When Grandpa Miller in Alabama
saw her down on the floor
clattering them around in uncounted stacks,
his eyes stretched wide
having always known
that money comes hard
and every cent counts
and some coins lie dormant for years
before their redeeming worth's revealed.
We gathered up a double handful
and put them in a plastic sack
for him to keep.

He slowly rolled each thick piece
between his bony finger and thumb
as though every nickel gram
were authentic gold or silver.
He just couldn't understand
that a pound of heavy coin
could be worth so little in U.S. cents.
He kept the bag hidden in a drawer
where he hoped no one would find and take
what so few knew to be of worth.
When Mother had to travel off with Dad
for a week away in California
to visit another grandson
he could hardly remember,
Grandpa Miller was taken to that strange place
of blaring TV and chanting women
and was roomed with another ancient man
who couldn't say what day it was.
His archaic suitcase carried only basic needs:
an electric razor dusted white with whiskers,
several days of underwear and socks,
pajamas, pants, a few shirts,
and the plastic bag with a pound of pesos
the nurse found and discretely handed over to me,
saying that she, "the home," and the staff
just couldn't take responsibility.

THE EMPTY SPACE AT THE HEAD OF THE TABLE
  —for Jack Dempsey

The empty space at the head of the table cannot be filled
nor can the dark hollowness in the pit of the aching heart.

The tobacco leaves harvested around Bardstown
turn brown and dry hung upside down and tied with twine
at their gathered stems to weathered two-by-two's
placed across rafters higher than ordinary men can climb
and fail to fill the massive emptiness of their barns.

The brackish water in Venice grows murky and rises
up the walls of the renaissance covering cobblestones
of open plazas like a shallow veil
contaminating fountains and slowing gondolas
to a drifting standstill because the push poles
no longer reach beneath the surface of their surroundings.

Fairways and greens resign themselves and surrender
to the invading overgrowth of saplings and weeds.
Another generation of canvasses leans unfinished
at its easels awaiting direction and advice. The very ink
has dried and disappeared from the yellowing pages
of a future chapbook of unwritten poems.

The empty space at the head of the table cannot be filled
even though the gathering at its edges grows
until the legs underneath buckle and fold
from the seeping overflow dripping from the surface.

THE SALVATORIAN
—*for Father Dominic*

The elderly priest has died in Wisconsin.
He went back to where he was ordained
sixty years before to spend his last days
in the company and care of the Merciful Sisters.

We didn't so much love him for his words
as much as for his silence.
                                    He could give
morning mass in less than forty minutes
and didn't try to impress the congregation
with his learning, his experience, or inspiration.
He impressed us being simple and brief.

His voice was sometimes reluctant to speak.
There would be an awkward pause
as he hacked to clear his throat
as though cutting through the superfluous,
the distractions concealing the essence and truth.

A few well-chosen words would finally come
but slow, weak and hoarse, between hard
breathing.
                    At the end of his brief homilies
he would take a seat, his robe draped over him
like a set of sails, and wait for the sanctuary
to fill with silence.
                            Even the smallest children
stayed quiet. Rays of colored light flowed in
through stained-glass windows.
                                    He would close
his eyes for long moments while the congregation
patiently awaited his next move.
                                  Some suspected
he fell asleep in those silent spaces of the mass.
Others thought he entered into another, deeper
state of consciousness: *the cloud of unknowing.*

During his last months at the rectory,
the other priest and the secretary said
he sat for hours staring into space
in utter silence.
                    When someone called it was
as though he snapped back from a distant place,
the place where he has now gone to stay,
to hover in the bliss of eternal quiet,
consumed forever into the cloud.

THE SCHOOL OF FISH
For Dorothy Hendry

In any school of fish
You have to look deep
And long to differentiate
The students from the teachers.

The leader takes her place
Inconspicuously amid the silver pack
Suspended steady and kept afloat
By uncountable invisible connections.

She honors the many threads
That hold them all together.
No matter how thin and frayed,
Faith in the union spawns strength.

She does not sink from the weight
Of worry and fear nor heed
Controlling rumors of impending
Invasions of predatory species.

Mother, daughter, sister, friend, and wife
To each and every fish who swims
Below as well as above,
She feeds on endless empathy.

She does not envy life on land
Nor dread the dome of air
Into which she will eventually ascend
But cherishes the awe and wonder of water

Where she admires the many treasures
Of her kingdom there, the hue
And texture of every swaying plant,
Idle stone and shifting sand;

And especially the other fish—
Her sibblings, daughters, students, sons.
Regardless of color, size, and shape
For them she kept swimming all these years.

MY GRANDPARENTS GAZE

                        from the bookshelves.
Papa, with his placid smile, his hair as white
as the shirt beneath his navy blue coat, stands
behind Mama's thick shoulder, her distant look
as pale and gray as the fading photograph.
Already they were late in life.
Mother and Aunt Marie insisted
on a portrait before it was too late.
They dissolve into the transparency of glass
and the black metal rim of the leaning frame.
It encloses them together
like their sixty years of matrimony,
a single inseparable life made of what
I never knew had ever been two.
Even their images are languishing like
corpses buried years ago, ghostly white
before a dull background of diminishing grief.
They stand before the spines of books
I procured at about the time the picture
was taken. Most I never took time to read,
but left waiting helpless for the vague promise
of my procrastination. They finally fade
into obsolescence, their message no news now
but history sinking fast into forgetting, dust
beginning to bury the edges of the pages,
the titles and authors' names
disappearing like tombstone inscriptions.
My grandparents stare like friendly spirits
from beyond the grave. It is the same
expression with which they greeted me
at their storybook house whenever I went
to visit in Glendale where quick summers
disappeared beneath the shade of hickories.

THE TRAIL

I found my own obscure trail
barely distinguishable amid
the underbrush and scattered leaves.
I stepped my way through swatting branches
that smacked no more than heavy air
since I followed no one
and no one came behind me.
I traveled light and carried
only the barest things I had
whose value I learned from struggle.
I meandered through the forest slowly,
taking my time, stopping to study
whatever appeared to be of interest.
Wandered off at times
but always kept the trail in sight
until one night I stopped to camp
just as the purple blanket of dark
with its sparkling stars and yellow moon
drew itself across the sky above the limbs.
I built a humble fire
just like on any other evening.
I didn't know that it would dissipate
like its own smoke while I slept
with my head upon a rock.
No angel came to wrestle.
No dream delivered visions.
I woke up staring at a blank white ceiling
hours later.   Or was it years?
I felt no panic throb inside my chest
but realized
with all too-patient resignation
that I had lost the trail, and yielded
to the most mundane of worlds.

HOPE

Just when you least expect
something good can happen.
Meteors do occasionally fall
lighting up an awful night
and acorns drop from naked trees.
It's a matter of standing there
thinly clad, waiting for
the frosty wind to cease.
Tides eventually turn.
Typhoons, floods and tropical storms
turn back and lumber out to sea
where no more houses can be blown down.
And yours is the very one that mustn't collapse.
It's got to dig in and hold
no matter where it's built—
no time now for geological tests—
sand, clay, and stone one and the same.
You've got to pull the roof
down over your windows
where only candle glow throbs within
and tilt your thin cracked shingles
toward the gusts that come but never last.
Who knows?
Some wailing wind might bring dollar bills
scattered among the leaves and tumbling papers.

THE MARIONETTE TANGO IN SAN TELMO

It is a cold gray Sunday afternoon in August
when the cobblestone plaza is packed
with antique vendors displaying crystal,
silverware, silver pesos, watches, clocks
and odd things whose use has been forgotten,
things that might have been brought from Spain,
Italy, England, Germany or France centuries before
or more-recently stolen from another neighborhood.

Vendors line the barricaded street
selling leather purses, wallets and belts,
knitted scarves and children's sweaters.
There are Peruvians selling wooden flutes,
Paraguayans embroidered blouses,
Columbians precious stones, Uruguayans
cured gourds with silver tubes for maté.
Andean quartets fill the air
with the distant hint of Asian sparrows.
Multiple accordions breathe melancholy tones.

The buildings side by side were private mansions
during the "Golden Age," but no one knows
when that might have been. Now mostly
subdivided into shops, principally antique
stores stuffed with the pawned
and discarded possessions that ebb and flow
during repeated cycles of hard times.
Of course, there are Italian restaurants,
meat grills, wine bars, and tired cafés.

On the sidewalk a puppeteer dressed
in charcoal gray suit and fedora hat
is pantomiming a song from a record
by Gardel as his hands dance before him
holding crosses tied with strings.
The marionette himself is dressed like the man
above who controls his every step,
bend, reach, and gesture, and seemingly
even the sad expression on his painted face.

The song's lyrics describe a man who has waited
all night for his partner to arrive at the wooden box
turned on its side and mocked to mimic
a little tango café and before it a street corner
with a lamp post in San Telmo years ago,
but the partner never comes and the marionette
keeps on drinking from a little black bottle
in one of his despondent little hands.

To the music of Gardel he tries to groove
into a solitary tango by himself, but by this time
he can hardly stand up because his feet keep
slipping out from under him. To the laughter
of the encircled audience gathered in the street,
he sways off balance with flailing arms
then topples off the edge of the little stage
but grabs hold with both hands, and after
assuring his grip, pauses to take another slug
from the little black bottle while dangling
by just one hand.

                First one knee, then the other,
he tries to throw a leg onto the precipice
from which he has fallen but keeps slipping
toward the abyss below we can only imagine.
He finally climbs onto the little street corner
on all fours as though praying or begging
his lost partner to return before, as Gardel sings
in the song, his own sorrow swallows him alive.

DARKNESS FALLS
—for Bruce Crowe

The Cicadas in Russellville
must be silent this summer
even though they rattle
like a thousand chains
across the rest of Alabama.
Cruel the irony
that you should leave
just when the grandchild
learns to hold a pencil.
Considerate as always,
you waited for your brother's
biannual visit from England.
The wife and daughter,
a mother now herself,
must have tried to prepare
as best they could.
No way to foresee
the last farewell
no matter how
they must have chided you
about the cigarettes
across the years,
so much a part
of the glow that we all know
and associate with you
as we gather like moths,
sometimes clumsy,
sometimes calm,
around your soft light
that will never disappear.

CAFÉ LA HABANA IN MEXICO CITY

The old buildings on Bucareli
have housed the city's major newspapers
—*El Excelcior, El Universal, La Jornada, El Sol*—
through years of revolution, volcano, earthquake,
and annual rains that flood streets over idle tires.
Café La Habana sits on the corner of *Avenida
Ayuntamiento* just as it has sat for over a century
with its half circle of counters, stools,
brass brewers, mahogany tables and chairs,
black and white photographic posters of the streets,
harbor, and *malecón* of old Havana
beneath which clients in Mexico can gaze
with nostalgia as they eat, sip coffee, and talk
about the sad situation of the country and the world.

It is the kind of place where Carlos Fuentes
and García Márquez met over stacks of open pages,
plates, saucers, cups, and discussed how there is
nothing more surreal and absurd than the daily news,
other tables occupied then by reporters,
correspondents, editors, printers, journalists,
and politicians. At another table in this very room
a young Che sat with Fidel and Raúl over *tortas*
and *tostones* to mark out the delivery of the island
to the people of its fields, drawing lines on a map
as cigar smoke intermingled with the aroma
of roasted coffee that remains today.
                                        The empty tables
have now grown to outnumber the occupied
—so many *compañeros* kidnapped, killed or disappeared.

COYOACÁN

                    is withering away without my feet
wandering through its labyrinth of streets.
The palmettos in the plaza still stand tall
but now their leaves stare down in sorrow
at black and gray pavement stones
where these two shoes no longer walk.

Along the edges of the streets gnarled limbs
of jacarandas and their trunks hunch over
like old women in tattered shawls
no longer able to keep count of mounting losses.

The thick walls of the houses,
their dull stucco painted yellow and orange
with the black wrought iron of their gates
and grillwork on dark windows,
stand stubborn and closed, refusing consolation,
in spite of blooming bougainvillea
drooping onto the outside world.

Even the glimmer inside the cathedral
slowly fades, dimming
the gilded woodwork of its arches, altars and domes.
In the middle of the afternoon
the frescoes on the ceiling and walls
seem veiled with dust and twilight shadow
as tears leak from the painted eyes of saints.

The restaurants and cafés wait
half-filled with empty tables.
The grieving sky darkens into purple
as long trains of taxis sit still
on the cobblestone streets
and defeated old men
hawk umbrellas from the curbs
prophesying yet another downpour.

THE PERFECT PLACE TO LIVE IN NEW ORLEANS

I found the perfect place
to live in New Orleans
on a flyer stuck to clapboard
beside the door
of the Creole Creamery
on Prytania Street Uptown:
for rent: one bedroom,
one bath, above the shop.
The idea of living on top
of all that ice cream
might not seem
perfect on its own
but The Wine Seller
waits aging on the corner
and next door,
The Chicory Expresso
with its almost-empty tables
whispers my name,
urging me to look within
and reclaim the life
I thought was lost.

THE SAME TABLE

I've been sitting at this table for forty years.
The *comadre's* food remains the same: the black *mole*,
the green salsa mixing with cream at the bottom of the plate,
the breaded pork chops, the chicken croquettes,
the diced papaya, the *agua de Jamaica*.

The same cobblestone patio lies beyond the glass
even though the sad jacaranda no longer slumps
weeping its shade across the stucco wall.

Though reupholstered years ago, these
are the same high-backed chairs that stood
so patiently around the oval table that afternoon
I first took my place amid the aroma
and the simultaneous conversations
I found so hard to follow.

Some of the people are the same,
but several have disappeared
through re-location, estrangement, divorce, or death.
Their children and grandchildren, wives
and husbands, girlfriends, nephews and nieces
reunite to occupy their predecessors' accustomed seats.

How much *café, chocolate* and *ron* have been poured
out before me here? How many ambiguous words
have risen with the smoke and floated in the room?

No matter how patiently these chairs wait,
like the glasses, they are eventually refilled.
The old aroma drifts from the kitchen
and even though so many of the voices
have sailed away like migratory birds
gone to another world, the rhythmic words
still rise like pigeons and flutter around the room.

James Miller Robinson has two previous chapbooks of poems: *The Caterpillars at Saint Bernard* (Mule on a Ferris Wheel Press) and *Boca del Río in the Afternoon* (Finishing Line Press). A graduate of the University of Alabama, he taught at Huntsville High School and in the Department of Foreign Languages and Literatures at the University of Alabama in Huntsville. He is currently a legal/court interpreter of Spanish registered with the Alabama Administrative Office of Courts and serves as an assistant editor of *POEM Magazine*. His work has appeared in *Southern Humanities Review, Texas Review, Xavier Review* and others.

www.ingramcontent.com/pod-product-compliance
Lightning Source LLC
LaVergne TN
LVHW041604070426
835507LV00011B/1298